phobias

phobias

things that **FREAK** *us out*

PENGUIN BOOKS

‘Tell us your phobias and we will tell you what you are afraid of.’

— *Robert Benchley*

acousticophobia fear of noise

agoraphobia fear of open spaces

aichurophobia fear of being touched by pointed objects

ailurophobia fear of cats

alektorophobia fear of chickens

alliumphobia fear of garlic

altophobia fear of heights

anglophobia fear of England or the English

anthophobia fear of flowers

anuptaphobia fear of staying single

arachibutyrophobia fear of getting peanut butter stuck to the roof of the mouth

arachnophobia fear of spiders

ballistophobia fear of being shot

barophobia fear of falling

batophobia fear of passing tall buildings

batrachophobia fear of frogs and toads

bibliophobia fear of books

brontophobia fear of thunder and lightning

bromidrosiphobia fear of body odour

cacophobia fear of ugliness

cacophonophobia fear of bad music

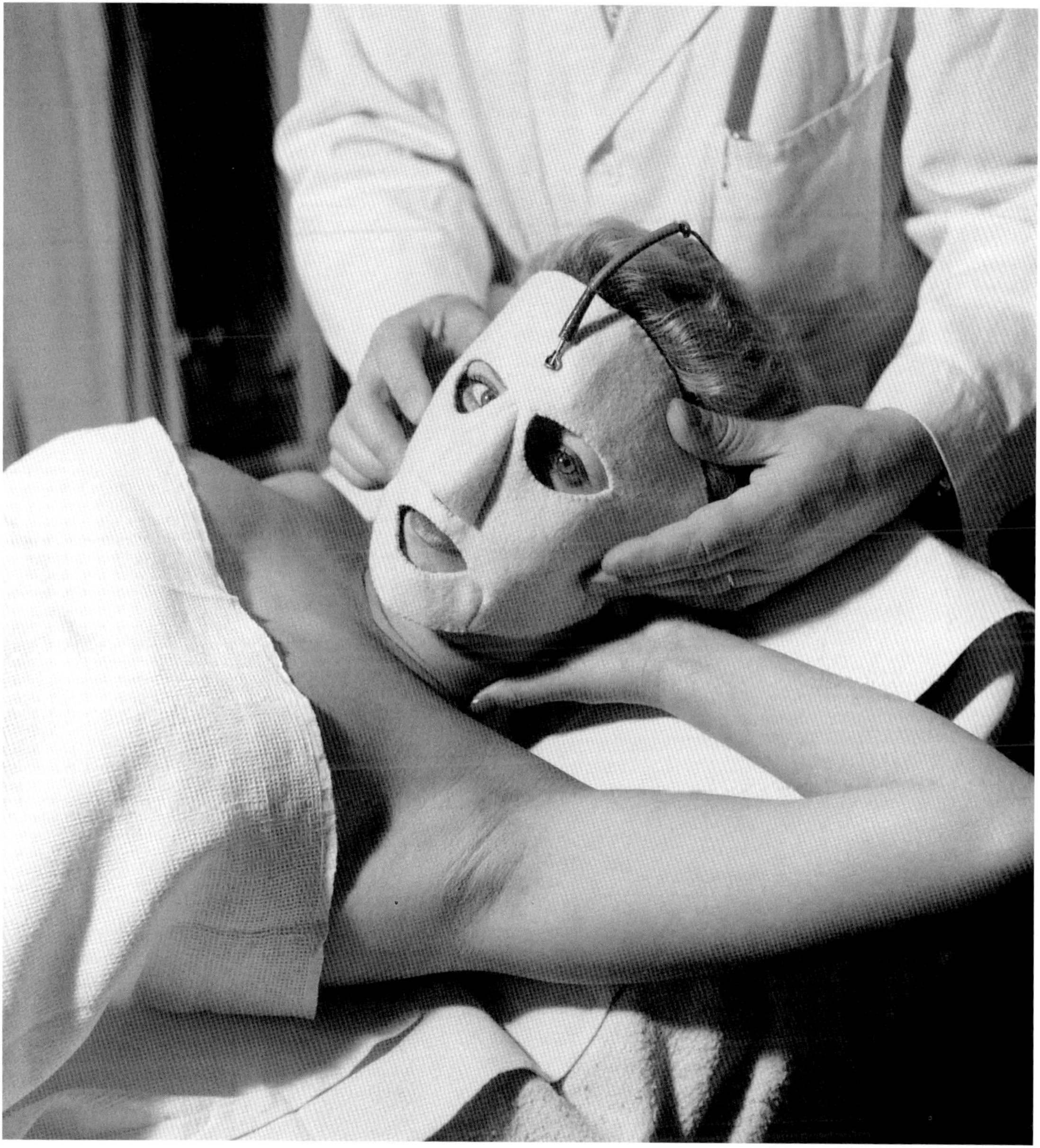

catagelophobia fear of being ridiculed

catapedaphobia fear of jumping

catoptrophobia fear of mirrors

chaetophobia (or **trichophobia**)
fear of hair

chorophobia fear of dancing

chromophobia fear of colours

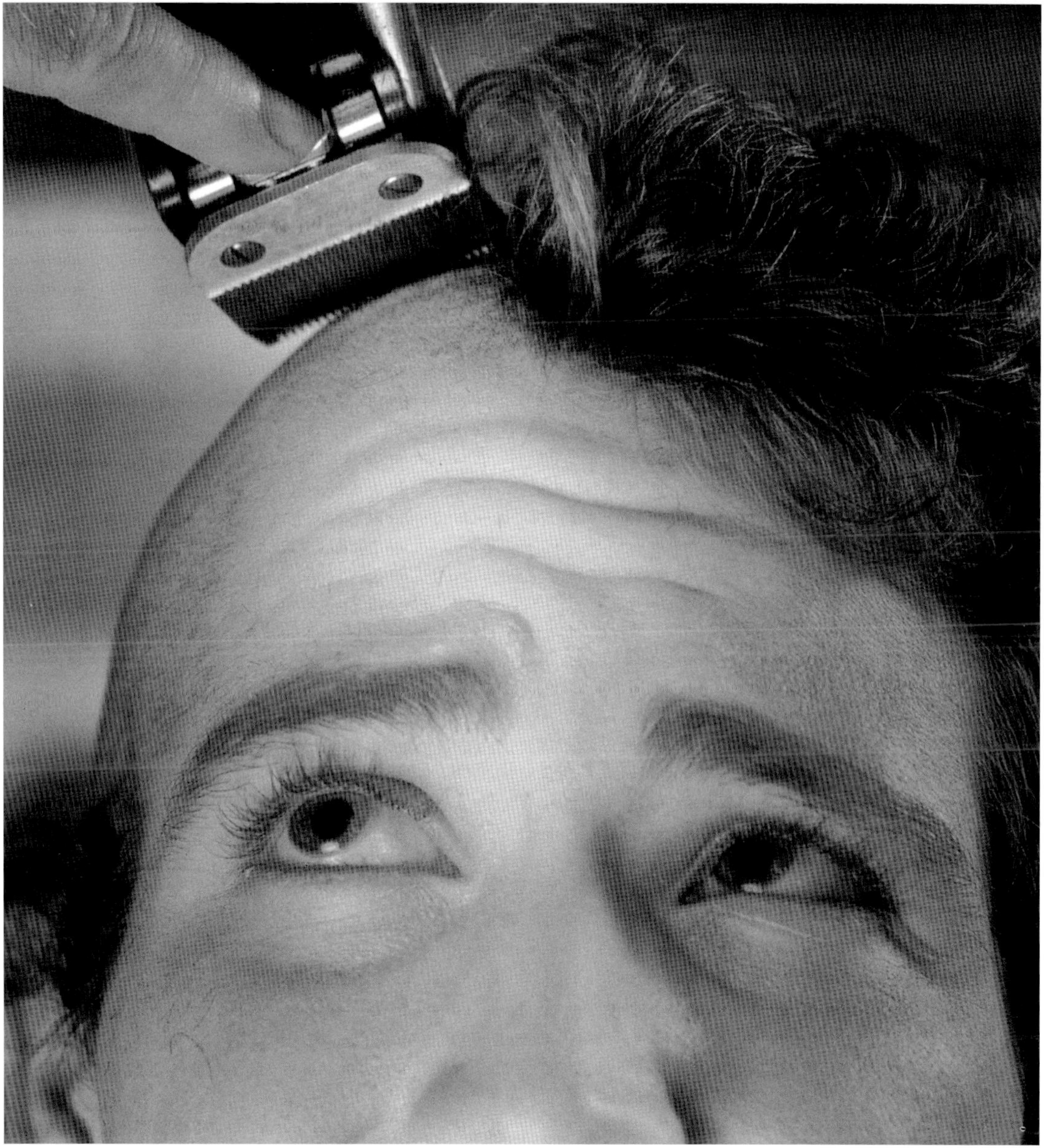

chronomentrophobia fear of clocks

claustrophobia fear of closed spaces

climacophobia fear of stairs

clinophobia fear of going to bed

coulrophobia fear of clowns

cyberphobia fear of computers

FATAL
ERROR

decidophobia fear of making decisions

didaskaleinophobia fear of going to school

dishabillophobia fear of undressing in front of others

dontophobia fear of dentists

dromophobia fear of crossing streets

dystycliphobia fear of accidents

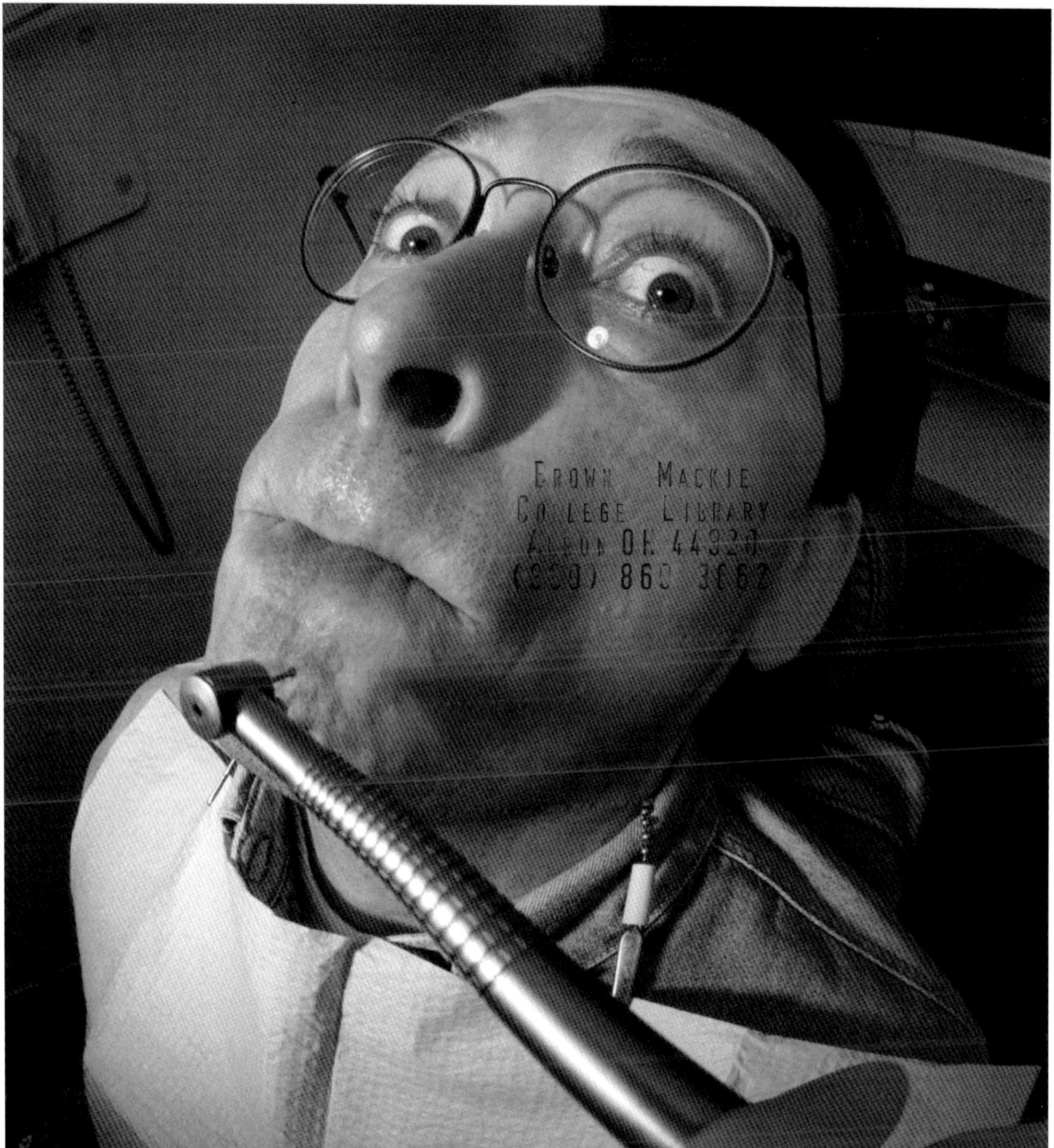

enetophobia fear of pins

entomophobia fear of insects

ephebiphobia fear of teenagers

epistaxiophobia fear of nosebleeds

epistemophobia fear of knowledge

ergasiophobia (or **ergophobia**) fear of work

erythrophobia fear of blushing

gamophobia fear of marriage

gelophobia fear of laughter

gelotophobia fear of being laughed at

geniophobia fear of chins

gephyrophobia fear of crossing bridges

gerontophobia fear of old people or old age

geumophobia fear of unfamiliar tastes

graphophobia fear of writing

gymnophobia fear of nudity

haphephobia fear of being touched

hedonophobia fear of pleasure

herpetophobia fear of reptiles or creepy-crawlies

heterophobia fear of the opposite sex

hippopotomonstrosesquippedaliophobia
fear of long words

hodophobia fear of travel

homophobia fear of sameness,
or of homosexuality

hypnophobia fear of sleep

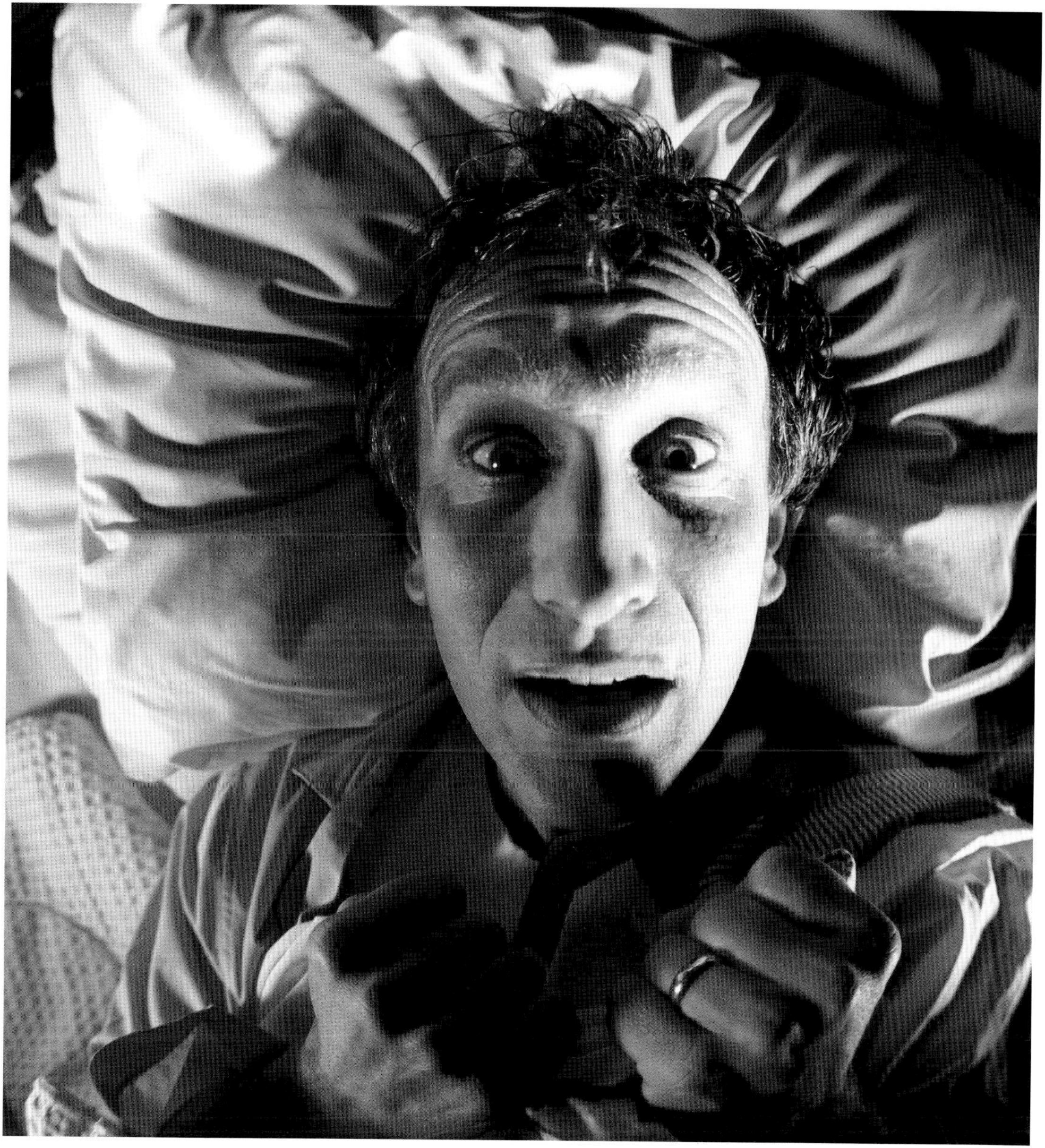

hypophobia absence of fear

ichthyophobia fear of fish

illyngophobia fear of vertigo
(feeling dizzy when looking down)

isolophobia fear of solitude, being alone

kakorrhaphiophobia fear of failure

kathisophobia fear of sitting down

koinoniphobia fear of rooms full of people

lachanophobia fear of vegetables

linonophobia fear of string

melanophobia fear of the colour black

melissophobia fear of bees

microbophobia fear of germs

microphobia fear of small things

musophobia fear of mice

myrmecophobia fear of ants

neophobia fear of anything new

nyctophobia fear of the dark

obesophobia fear of gaining weight

oenophobia fear of wines

olfactophobia fear of odours

omophagiaphobia fear of eating raw flesh

ophidophobia fear of snakes

optophobia fear of opening one's eyes

ornithophobia fear of birds

ovophobia fear of eggs

pantophobia fear of everything

papaphobia fear of the Pope

papyrophobia fear of paper

paronomasiaphobia fear of puns

pediophobia fear of children

peladophobia fear of baldness

phagophobia fear of eating

phasmaphobia fear of ghosts

phengophobia fear of daylight or sunshine

philemaphobia fear of kissing

phobophobia fear of fearing

photophobia fear of having one's photograph taken

pogonophobia fear of beards

policophobia fear of the police

politicophobia fear or abnormal dislike of politicians

polyphobia fear of many things

potophobia fear of alcoholic drink

psellismophobia fear of stuttering

pteromerhanophobia fear of flying

pteronophobia fear of being tickled by feathers

rhinophobia fear of noses

rhytiphobia fear of wrinkles

scelerophobia fear of bad men

sciophobia fear of shadows

selachophobia fear of sharks

socerophobia fear of one's parents-in-law

stenophobia fear of narrow places

symmetrophobia fear of symmetry

tachophobia fear of speed

taphephobia fear of being buried alive

taurophobia fear of bulls

textophobia fear of certain fabrics

thalassophobia fear of the sea

thanatophobia fear of death

traumatophobia fear of injury

tryapanophobia fear of injections

vacansopapurosophobia fear of blank paper

venustraphobia fear of beautiful women

verbophobia fear of words

vermiphobia fear of worms

vestiophobia fear of clothing

SCARED

wiccaphobia fear of witches

xanthophobia fear of the colour yellow

xenophobia fear of foreigners or strangers

xerophobia fear of dryness or dry places

xylophobia fear of forests or wood

zoophobia fear of animals

PENGUIN BOOKS

Published by the Penguin Group
Penguin Group (Australia)
250 Camberwell Road, Camberwell, Victoria 3124, Australia
(a division of Pearson Australia Group Pty Ltd)
Penguin Group (USA) Inc.
375 Hudson Street, New York, New York 10014, USA
Penguin Group (Canada)
90 Eglinton Avenue East, Suite 700, Toronto, Canada, ON M4P 2Y3
(a division of Pearson Penguin Canada Inc.)
Penguin Books Ltd
80 Strand, London WC2R 0RL England
Penguin Ireland
25 St Stephen's Green, Dublin 2, Ireland
(a division of Penguin Books Ltd)
Penguin Books India Pvt Ltd
11 Community Centre, Panchsheel Park, New Delhi – 110 017, India
Penguin Group (NZ),
67 Apollo Drive, Mairangi Bay, Auckland 1310, New Zealand
(a division of Pearson New Zealand Ltd)
Penguin Books (South Africa) (Pty) Ltd
24 Sturdee Avenue, Rosebank, Johannesburg 2196, South Africa

Penguin Books Ltd, Registered Offices: 80 Strand, London, WC2R 0RL, England

First published by Penguin Group (Australia), 2006

10 9 8 7 6 5 4 3 2 1

Photographs pp. 21, 55 Alamy Images; pp. 33, 77, 89 APL/Corbis; 3, 5, 11, 13, 15, 19, 23, 25, 27, 29, 35, 37, 41, 45, 47, 49, 51, 53, 57, 63, 65, 67, 71, 75, 79, 81, 85, 87 Getty Images; pp. 43, 61, 73 Jupiterimages; pp. 7, 9, 17, 31, 39, 59, 69, 83, 91 photolibrary.com

Cover and text design by Elizabeth Theodosiadis © Penguin Group (Australia)
Cover photograph reproduced by permission of Universal Studios
Produced by the Australian Book Connection

ISBN-13: 978 0 14 300547 6
ISBN-10: 0 14 30054 72

Cataloguing information about this book is available from the National Library of Australia

www.penguin.com.au